SCIENTOLOGY
Making the World a Better Place

GH00374900

Founded and developed by L. Ron Hubbard, Scien eligious philosophy which offers an exact route throug.. w.......u anyone can egain the truth and simplicity of his spiritual self.

Scientology consists of specific axioms that define the underlying causes and principles of existence and a vast area of observations in the humanities, a philosophic body that literally applies to the entirety of life.

This broad body of knowledge resulted in two applications of the subject: first, a technology for man to increase his spiritual awareness and attain the freedom sought by many great philosophic teachings; and, second, a great number of fundamental principles men can use to improve their lives. In fact, in this second application, Scientology offers nothing less than practical methods to better *every* aspect of our existence—means to create new ways of life. And from this comes the subject matter you are about to read.

Compiled from the writings of L. Ron Hubbard, the data presented here is but one of the tools which can be found in *The Scientology Handbook*. A comprehensive guide, the handbook contains numerous applications of Scientology which can be used to improve many other areas of life.

In this booklet, the editors have augmented the data with a short introduction, practical exercises and examples of successful application.

Courses to increase your understanding and further materials to broaden your knowledge are available at your nearest Scientology church or mission, listed at the back of this booklet.

Many new phenomena about man and life are described in Scientology, and so you may encounter terms in these pages you are not familiar with. These are described the first time they appear and in the glossary at the back of the booklet.

Scientology is for use. It is a practical philosophy, something one *does*. Using this data, you *can* change conditions.

Millions of people who want to do something about the conditions they see around them have applied this knowledge. They know that life can be improved. And they know that Scientology works.

Use what you read in these pages to help yourself and others and you will too.

CHURCH OF SCIENTOLOGY INTERNATIONAL

*P*ublic relations provides the means to communicate your ideas and get them accepted—a skill vitally necessary when dealing with new ideas. It is a way to gain support for your projects and endeavors.

Generally considered a method to gain publicity, public relations has previously been subjected to severe limitations. This was a practice that lacked certain key elements. Now, because of some important discoveries in Scientology, advances have made the entire activity significantly more useful and effective.

L. Ron Hubbard's refinement of public relations not only makes it essential for any group and any individual, but removes the previously inherent limitations. Although the full technology is extensive, the basic principles covered here will be of immense value to anyone with a worthwhile purpose.■

PUBLIC RELATIONS

W hen one is dealing with others to gain their agreement or cooperation or support for something, he has entered the field of public relations, or PR for short.

The definition of PR is: GOOD WORKS WELL PUBLICIZED.

Doing good works is not enough, one has to actually publicize it to gain cooperation or agreement.

In public relations one is essentially reaching people with an idea of some kind and gaining their agreement. One's success in dealing with others, then, is effective to the degree that he can reach them with the idea he intends them to have.

Public relations is an indispensable tool to help one get his ideas across, and any person who is making the world a better place would benefit greatly from its use.

No matter what you do—from taking actions to improve education in an area, to helping people get off drugs—by using the tools of public relations you can reach others with the correct message and gain their agreement on it. Thus it opens the door to acceptance of the activity you want to do.

Public relations is not new. It existed as a formal subject in Roman times, when it was employed for the purpose of electing senators. Even then, political campaign slogans were written on the walls of the Colosseum for people to see.

Through the centuries PR has remained only partially developed as a subject, suppressed in its development by the ill-intentioned who were only interested in using it to serve their ulterior motives.

It wasn't until Scientology, with its discoveries about communication and the true nature of man, that public relations actually became a complete subject of benefit to the society and to the individual.

Public relations is a technology. It has its own laws.

To begin to learn the techniques of public relations, you must start with an understanding of the basic factors or ingredients which make up the subject.

*No matter
how effective
a program is…*

…it may not
be successful if one
cannot achieve
cooperation and
wide agreement
for it.*

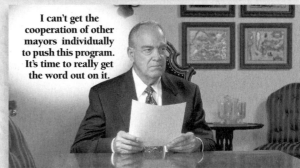

*But using the
technology of
public relations…*

…one can succeed
in his endeavors
and accomplish his
aims more rapidly.*

The Missing Ingredient

There has been a missing ingredient in the technology of public relations for as long as this subject has existed. This omission has been one of the key factors that has rendered public relations incomplete as a subject and, consequently, something of potential liability to its user.

This ingredient is *reality*.

The things which we perceive with our senses are real. Reality is essentially *agreement* upon perceptions and data in the physical universe. It is the degree of agreement reached between people. You are either in agreement with your fellows or in disagreement with your fellows, and as you agree or disagree, thus is your reality.

Those things upon which you and your fellows agree are real. Those things upon which you disagree are not real.

It was discovered in Scientology that reality is interconnected with two other components: affinity and communication.

The term *affinity* is fairly close in meaning to the word *like*. However, affinity is a two-way proposition. Not only do you *like* something but you feel that it likes you. Affinity is also very much like the word *love* when *love* is used in the universal sense. It includes both *love* and *like* and is broader than both.

Communication is the interchange of ideas across space. A man's impact on the world has been directly proportionate to his development of a means of communication. Communication in its broadest sense, of course, includes all the ways in which a person or thing becomes aware of, or becomes aware to, another person or thing.

These three components—affinity, reality and communication—form the ARC (pronounced A-R-C) triangle of Scientology and together these form the component parts of understanding.

If one corner of this triangle (say A) is raised, the other two will rise. If one corner is lowered, the other two are as well.

Thus with high affinity, one also has a high reality and a high communication. With a low affinity one has also a low reality and a low communication.

With a high or low R one has a high or low A and C.

And so it goes. The whole triangle rises and lowers as one piece. One cannot have a low R and a high A and C.

Public relations is supposed to be a *communication* technique. I communicates ideas. Suppose one were to try to communicate an out-the bottom R. In such a case the communication would possibly at first reach, bu then it would recoil due to its R.

This whole interrelationship of affinity, reality and communication is o course an advance in the technology of Scientology. It was not available to early pioneers of PR. So they talked (and still talk) mainly lies.

Older PR practitioners *preferred* lies. They used circus exaggeration o covert attacks using slander and falsehoods on persons' reputations. They sought to startle or intrigue and the easiest way to do it was with exclamatior point "facts" which were in fact lies.

"Mental health" public relations men dreamed up out of whole cloth the "statistics" of the insane. "Nine out of every fifteen Englishmen will go insane at some period of their lives" is a complete lie. Streams of such false statistic: gush from PR lobbyists to get a quick pound from Parliament.

The stock in trade of public relations people, whether hired by Stalin Hitler, the US president or the International Bank, has been black, baldfaced lies.

A US president once gave two different figures of the percentage o increased government cost per year in two months. His public relations mar was trying to influence Congress.

The "Backfire 8" as the "Car of the Century" and the parachute exhibitior "record delayed drop" and the ambassador's press conference on "Middle Eas Aims" are all public relations functions—and salted throughout with lies.

You pick up a newspaper or listen in the street and you see PR—PR—PR– all lies.

A battle cruiser makes a "goodwill visit" to a town it is only equipped t crush and you have more lies.

The tremendous power of newspapers, magazines, radio, TV and moder "mass media" communication is guided by the PR men of special interests an they guide with lies.

Thus public relations is corrupted to "a technique of lying convincingly."

It makes a cynical world. It has smashed idealism, patriotism and morality. Why?

When an enforced communication channel carries only lies, then the ffinity caves in and you get hate. For the R is corrupted.

Public relations, dedicated to a false reality of lies, then becomes low A, w C and recoils on the user.

So the first lesson we can learn that enables us to use PR safely is to KEEP . HIGH R.

The more lies you use in public relations the more likely it is that the PR ill recoil.

Thus the law:

NEVER USE LIES IN PR.

The trouble with public relations then was its lack of *reality*. A lie of course a false reality.

The trouble with PR was R!

In getting out a press release on a new can opener that opens cans easily, nd you want to say "A child could use it," find out if it's a fact. Give one to a hild and have him open a can. So it's true. So use the line and say what child. on't call it the "Can Opener of the Century." It won't communicate.

Just because radios, TVs and press pour out does not mean they ommunicate. Communication implies that somebody is reached.

Any lie will either blunt the C (communication) or end the C off one day ith revulsion.

So there *is* a technique known as public relations. And it has the high ability of abuse through lies and the degrade of its practitioner.

But if one strictly attends to the values of truth and affinity, he will be able communicate and can stand up to the strain.

Knowing this, public relations becomes a far more useful and mature bject.

The next thing to know about this is "who" or what "public" one is trying communicate with. Lack of this knowledge can lead to fruitless public lations efforts.

PUBLICS

What is a "public"?

One hears "*the* public," a star says "*my* public." You look in the dictionar
and you find "public" means an organized or general body of people.

There is a specialized definition of the word "*public*" which is not in th
dictionary but which is used in the field of public relations. "*Public*" is
professional term to public relations people. It doesn't mean the mob or th
masses. It means "a *type of audience.*"

The broad population to PR professionals is divided up into separat
publics. Possibly the early pioneers in public relations should have begun t
use "audiences" back in 1911 when some of the first texts on PR were writter
But they didn't. They used the word "publics" to mean different types o
audiences for their communications.

So you won't find this in the dictionaries as a public relations profession:
term. But you sure better wrap your wits and tongue around this term for us•
Otherwise, you'll make more PR errors than can easily be computered.

Wrong public sums up about 99 percent of the errors in public relation
activities and adds up to the majority reason for PR failures.

So what's a "public"?

In PRese (public relations slang) use "public" along with another wor
always. There is no single word form for "public" in public relations. A publi
relations professional never says THE public.

There is the "community public," meaning people in the town not personal
grouped into any other special public. There is the "employee public," meanir
the people who work for the firm. There's the "shareholder public," meaning th
people who own shares in the company. There's the "teenage public," meaning th
under-twenty people. There's the "doctor public," meaning the MD audience or
is trying to reach.

There are hundreds of different types of publics.

An interest in common or a professional or social class characteristic i
common—some similarity amongst a special group—determines the type o
public or audience.

Employee Public	Teenage Public	Doctor Public

A person applying public relations needs this grouping as he can expect each different type of public to have different interests. Therefore his promotion to them must be designed especially for each type of public.

In the public relations world there aren't kids—there is a "child public." There aren't teenagers—there's a "teenage public." There aren't elderly people—there's an "elderly public."

Someone using public relations does not think in huge masses. He thinks in group types within the masses.

Public relations is an activity concerned with *presentation* and *audience*. Even when he writes a news release, he "slants" it for a publication that reaches a type of audience and he writes it *for* that audience.

In order to do this, he first has to have an idea of the opinions or reality of that public or audience. He finds that out by conducting a survey.

A *survey* is a sampling, or partial collection, of facts, figures or opinions taken and used to approximate or indicate what a complete collection and analysis might reveal.

For instance, there is a group of three thousand teachers in one area and you want to find out what they want from the school board. By asking two hundred of those teachers, selected at random, you can get a good idea of where the whole group of teachers stands on that particular question.

"Public" is a professional term to PR people. It doesn't mean the mob or the masses. It means "a type of audience."

A user of PR techniques *surveys* in terms of special publics. Then h presents his material so as to influence *that* particular public.

He doesn't offer stories about wheelchairs to the teenage public or Micke Mouse prizes to the elderly public.

All things being offered to the public should be designed to reach a specia public.

When you mix it up, you fail.

When you get it straight and survey it, you succeed.

Someone who did not understand this concept of publics could mis completely. If some PR man tried to promote the "praises of John Dillinger to the "police public," he would certainly not get a response. Likewise, th "criminal public" isn't going to go into raptures over the "heroes in blue"!

All expert public relations is aimed at a specific, carefully surveyed, specia audience called a "_____ public."

When you know that, you can grasp the subject of public relations.

When you can use it expertly, you are a professional in the field of publi relations.

Anyone using PR has to figure out his precise publics. There may b several distinct types.

Then he has to survey and look over the reactions of each different type.

He then plans and designs his communication and offerings for each on

He sends the right message to the right public in each case. There may b a dozen different messages if there are a dozen different publics. Each one i right for that public.

Someone using public relations is after a result, a call-in, a reply, response.

The right message in the right form to the right public gets the result.

A wrong message to the wrong public simply costs lots of money and ge no result.

Knowing the right public, one can then survey them and communicate t them with reality.

If you want to obtain results, know who your publics are.

SURVEYS

As you read earlier in this booklet, it is important to use reality in PR and to know the reality level of the public you are addressing.

Surveys accomplish this.

In public relations terminology, "survey" means to carefully examine public opinion with regard to an idea, a product, an aspect of life or any other subject. By examining in detail (person to person surveying) one can arrive at a whole view of public opinion on a subject by tabulating highest percentage of popular response.

But what does this mean to an individual on his own? Certainly he cannot rush out and hire polling experts or a research company to tell him all about the neighbors in the new neighborhood he just moved into or what students think in class or what fellow employees at work think about his project.

The fact is, a person can do his own surveys very easily.

A survey is done in order to find what *buttons* a group has. In surveying, the word *button* means the subject or phrase or concept that communicates the reality of a specific public. It is something that is real to the majority of persons in that group and which can be used to get a response and gain agreement. The term came from the early 1900s expression "press the button" which means, in a figurative sense, "to perform an action that automatically brings about the required state of affairs." In public relations the state of affairs one wants is agreement and cooperation with one's actions.

In a survey, you question people to get their opinion on something. A *button* is the primary datum you get from this action. It is the answer given the most number of times to your survey question. It is what will elicit agreement and response.

Surveys can also be designed to tell you what people detest.

With a knowledge of a public's reality as gained through surveys, one has opened the door to informing them of the ideas one wants them to accept— in other words he can get his *message* across.

The *message* is the communication, the thought, the significance you want to get across to an audience or public.

A *button* is used to get the public's agreement to hear the message.

A message and a button are *not* the same thing.

By doing a survey and finding the right button, you can then use that button to elicit agreement and thereby get response.

To do a proper survey and to then use its results effectively requires an understanding of the purpose of surveys, and of ARC and the ARC triangle. It requires an understanding of what reality is.

One uses the ARC triangle in conducting a survey initially and, following that, one applies the ARC triangle in putting the survey results to use.

It goes like this: One *communicates* to an audience or public (via a survey) with *affinity* to find out what the *reality* of that audience is. Reality is agreement as to what is. The reason you do a survey is to find out what that audience or public will agree with.

One then approaches the public with that *reality* in a promotional piece or some other communication to get the public's agreement to hear the message. And thus one raises the public's *affinity* for the item one is promoting.

That is the simplicity of it. But it will only be simple to the person who understands the ARC triangle. Without reality or some agreement communication will not reach and affinity will be absent.

Thus, surveys are done to get agreement. Surveys are not done for any other purpose. They're done to establish agreement with an audience.

You ask ten or ten hundred people what they would most want or expect of an automobile tire and seven or seven hundred of them tell you

SURVEY EXAMPLE

Here is an example of an actual survey. A group of Scientologists in South Africa was interested in finding out how best to reach children in rural townships with an educational program using Scientology Study Technology. They saw that in order to do this they first needed to determine what children considered to be the major barriers facing them.

The questions asked and the top answers with their percentages were:

1. Who do you take advice from?

73% Parents

13% Brother or sister

5% Teacher

2. What do you feel is the biggest problem in the world today?

50% Violence, war

15% Nothing, no problem

10% Education

3. What could be done to change that?

23% Stop it

15% Nothing, no problem

10% Education

4. What in your life would you like to change the most?

25% Violence, hatred

18% The situation, everything

15% Education

5. What in your life is going the best?

33% Education

30% Nothing

15% Everything

6. What thing in your life do you look forward to the most?

58% School, education

10% Don't know

10% Everything, anything

"durability." That's the button. That's the reality, the point of agreement on automobile tires among that public. So you use that button with that public and you've established reality; you've got agreement and they will then listen to what you have to say about automobile tires.

Buttons have their use but we are not so much interested in them as we are in *message*. The message is the real essence of any promotional piece or PR communication. Buttons are just the grease to use to get your message through.

A survey like the one in the example just given would be of great use in reaching children with tools by which they can learn and receive a meaningful education.

Buttons found from the survey include:

Parents—these children listen to their parents.

Violence, war—this came up as their biggest problem and something they would most like to change.

Education and school was the part of their lives which they most look forward to.

Having conducted such a survey, the results could then be used by this group to get their program better known and accepted. Their basic message is that workable methods of education exist and will help them. Using these survey results they could state their message so it would be better accepted. They could say, for example, "Education is the solution to violence and a better life for you, and our program will help you get a valuable education."

How to Conduct a Survey

The actions involved in doing a survey are simple and few. The first thing is to establish the questions you are going to ask the public to find out what is wanted and needed, popular or unpopular or whatever.

After the questions are established, they are written or typed on a piece of plain paper for the surveyor to refer to. If one were doing a survey in a city where large numbers of people were interviewed, survey forms might be most practical. However, all that is needed for most surveys is a clipboard with plenty of plain paper and several ballpoint pens (so running out of ink in the middle of the survey doesn't cause interruption). The survey question page is then placed on top of the pad of paper and flipped back while taking notes of the interview.

To begin a survey, you simply walk up to a person and in a friendly manner introduce yourself (if a stranger) and ask to survey them. If the person asks for more information about the survey or why it is being done, his questions are answered and the survey is begun.

Ask the person the first question, flip back the question page and take down the answer. Be sure to number the answers corresponding to the question number being asked. You needn't write down every word as the person speaks to you, but get the most important points. You will find, after practice surveying, you can write almost everything down.

After the person has answered the first question, thank him or her and go to the next question.

At the end of the survey, thank the person. The person will most likely be thanking you at this point as people love to be asked their opinion of things. And having another person listen attentively is a rare and valuable experience to many.

Then go to the next person and repeat the same procedure. This is all there is to the mechanical action of surveying.

Tabulation of Surveys

Once a survey is done, the responses have to be tabulated in order to b usable.

The word "tabulate" is defined by *Webster's New World Dictionary* as, "t put (facts, statistics, etc.) in a table or columns; arrange systematically."

In tabulating survey responses, you are arranging the data gathere systematically in order to permit analysis of those results. The definition c "analysis" could be stated as "examination in detail so as to determine th nature or tendencies of."

The most commonly used format for survey tabulations is to list eac question, with the categories of responses and their percentages laid out fror highest percentage to lowest under each question.

In order to accomplish public relations that are effective and whic communicate one's message and make one's good works well known, it i essential that one know what his publics want or will accept, what they wi agree with and what they will believe.

Surveys, then, give one the reality of one's public. Without them, one i going at it blindly in a hit-or-miss fashion that will not get him very far.

TABULATION PROCEDURE

1. Count all the surveys.

2. Establish various categories of answers for each question by listing answers briefly but accurately as you go through the survey responses.

3. When categories have been established, you will be able to simply mark a slant next to the appropriate category, meaning one more answer of a similar nature.

4. Once all the responses have been tabulated, count up the number of responses in each category for each question.

5. Work out the percentage for each category under each question. This is done by dividing the number of surveys and multiplying by 100. Let's say you had 1,500 answers of a similar nature to one question and your total number of surveys is 2,500.

$$1,500 \div 2,500 = 0.6 \times 100 = 60$$

This means 60 percent gave that similar type of answer.

6. The only mistake you can make is not to realize the similarity of answers and so have a great diversity of categories.

A survey is done so that you elicit response and agreement.

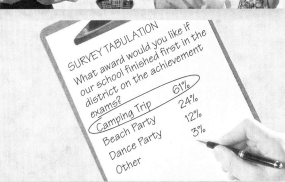

Agreement is obtained by finding and then using the right button.

With the reality established a plan can be communicated…

…which will gain acceptance and cooperation.

How to Handle Rumors and Whispering Campaigns

There may be times when one's reputation comes under attack by rumo or gossip, giving one a false reality and making him unreal and out o agreement with the people he is in contact with. This situation is the opposit of what good public relations is supposed to accomplish. It amounts to "ba works falsely publicized."

Often a person just shrugs and accepts this as part of life; this is the way i is and there is no trusting human nature. Others bitterly fight to defend thei reputations and, lacking the technology of public relations that can show on how to deal with such circumstances, go about it in such a way that thei denials only make matters worse.

Slander does not just happen to celebrities or political figures. Rumors an lies can make life unpleasant in any social circle.

What does one do when threatened with such attacks upon one's goo name?

There are standard public relations solutions to this problem that on should know and apply if this type of situation ever arises.

"Black propaganda" (black = bad or derogatory; propaganda = pushing ou statements or ideas) is the term used to describe the technique employed t destroy reputation or public belief in persons, companies or nations.

The technique of black propaganda seeks to bring a reputation so low tha the person, company or nation is denied any rights whatever by "genera agreement." It is then possible to destroy the person, company or nation wit a minor attack if the black propaganda itself has not already accomplished his.

Vicious and lying gossip by old women was the earlier form of this tactic and was so bad that some areas put them in public stocks (neck yokes) or drove them out of town.

In modern times there is no such check on black propaganda. Difficulties and costs of libel and slander suits, abuse of press privilege, and so forth, lay anyone open to such a campaign.

All one needs is an enemy. And there are few men in history who have been without enemies.

There are random individuals in the society who do not understand very much.

This is expressed as a sort of malicious glee about things. Such pass on slanderous rumors very easily. In an illiterate society such people abound. Since they cannot read, the bulk of knowledge is denied to them. Since they do not know very many words, much of what is said to them is not understood.

This is not isolated to the illiterate only.

What they do not understand they substitute for with imaginary things.

Thus such persons not only listen to slander but also corrupt and twist even it.

Thus a rumor can go through a society that has no basis in truth.

When numbers of such rumors exist and are persistent, one suspects a "whispering campaign." This is not because people whisper these things but because like an evil wind it *seems* to have no source.

Black propaganda makes use of such a willingness to pass on and amplify falsehoods.

Much black propaganda is of course more bold and appears blatantly in irresponsible (or covertly controlled) newspapers and radio and television.

But even after a bad press story has appeared or a bad radio or TV broadcast has been given, the "whispering campaign" is counted upon by black propagandists to carry the slander through the society.

Thus any person, any being, is at risk.

A person comes to fear bad things being said about him. In the face of a whispering campaign, real or imagined, one tends to withdraw, tends to become less active and reach less.

This is equally true of companies and even nations.

Thus, unless one knows how to handle such an attack, one can in fact be made quite miserable and ill.

The Law of the Omitted Data

There is a natural law at work that unfortunately favors black propaganda.

WHERE THERE IS NO DATA AVAILABLE PEOPLE WILL INVENT IT.

This is the Law of the Omitted Data.

A vacuum tends to fill itself. Old philosophers said that "nature abhors a vacuum." Actually the surrounding pressure flows into an area of no pressure.

It is this way with a person, company or nation.

Hit by lies the person tends to withdraw. This already tends to pull things in.

The person does not then wish to put out data. He becomes to some degree a mystery.

To fill that mystery people will invent data.

This is true of persons, companies or nations.

This is where *public relations is a necessity.*

Essentially public relations is the art of making good works well known.

It is a fatal error to think good works speak for themselves. They do not. They must be publicized.

Essentially this is what public relations is. And this is *why* it is—to fill that vacuum of omitted data. In the midst of a black propaganda campaign one is denied normal communication channels. The press media along which the campaign is being conducted will *not* run favorable comment. One is mad if he thinks it will as it is serving other masters that mean to destroy the repute of the target.

"Authoritative" utterances push plain truth out of sight.

Thus public relations people have to be very expert in their technology when they confront black propaganda.

The Handling

When one is not fighting a battle against black propaganda, public relations is easy.

One hires a reporter who gets to work thinking up ideas and turning out releases. That's why reporters are often thought of as public relations people, which they are not.

In the face of a black propaganda campaign, such releases are twisted, refused and that is the end of it.

There is far more to the art than this.

These are some of the rules that apply:

Fill the Vacuum

First of all, cease to withdraw. It is proven conclusively that in public relations handling of black propaganda, only the outflow of information pays off. Saying nothing may be noble in a character but it is fatal in public relations.

Blunt denial is crude and can be used against one as a sort of confirmation.

You don't have to announce or spread a flap and never should. Public relations men often *make* the flap.

But don't interpret this as "silence is necessary." Get in a safe place and speak up.

Use any channel to speak up. But don't seek channels that will corrupt what you say in repeating it.

Don't stay on the same subject that you are being attacked on.

An example of speaking up without denying and thus confirming might be

STATEMENT: "I read your company went broke last month."

REBUTTAL: "My God. You're telling me! If we hadn't got out of that contract we really would have gone broke. There was a hell of a row in the boardroom. But McLinty won. Scotch to the core. He said, 'I won't sign it! Like to have tore the president's head off. Hell of a row. Seems like we got 80 million buried somewhere and McLinty is in charge of it and he won't *move an inch* on it."

The interrogator's conclusion is you're not broke. He's got data. The vacuum is filled with a story of board rows and 80 million mysterious reserves.

Disprove False Data

This consists of disproving utterly the false statement with documents or demonstration or display. One has to have a kit (a collection of documents) or the ability to demonstrate or something to display.

STATEMENT: "I've been told you are in trouble with the County Board of Health."

REBUTTAL: "Here's our recently issued health certificate and a letter of commendation from the Board of Health." Displays same.

Result? Whoever told him that is now discredited with him as an accurate informer.

When the person makes some disprovable statement, find *who* to fix his mind on it and then produce the rebuttal.

STATEMENT: "I hear you aren't married to the man you're living with."

REBUTTAL: "*Who* told you that?"

STATER: "I forget."

REBUTTER: "Well, you remember and I'll show you some proof."

STATER: "Well, it was a man...."

REBUTTER: *"Who?"*

STATER: "Joe Schmo."

REBUTTER: "Okay. Here's my marriage certificate. Who's the Joe Schmo nut anyway?"

Now it's Joe Schmo who's the mystery. How come he lies? What's in it for him?

When one hasn't got the document but can get it, one can say, "You tell me the name of whoever said that and next time I see you I'll show you something *very* interesting about it."

And be sure to get the document and see him again.

There are a billion variations. "It won't fly." Fly it. "Place is empty." Show him it's full.

The subject matter of this is *proof* in whatever form.

You only challenge statements you *can* prove are false and in any conversation let the rest slide.

Disprove Every Rumor

Proving negatives is almost impossible. "How do I know you aren't a CIA man?" Well, how can one prove that? One can't whip out a KGB badge as that would be just as bad. No one ever wrote a document, "Bill Till is not a member of the CIA." Useless. It is a denial. Who'd believe it?

Sometimes "You don't" works.

But the right answer to a negative (no proof) is to "fill the vacuum."

And once in a while you *can* prove a negative. Accused of drug smuggling one can show he's a member of the antidrug league. The counter in a negative proof must be *creditable.*

A million million variations exist.

Where there is no data available people will invent it. This law unfortunately favors black propaganda.

If the vacuum is filled by true data…

…the black propaganda is seen to be a lie and vanishes.

The basis of it is *not* to be the thing rumored and to be able to prove it fast.

Continue to Fill the Vacuum

Continuous good works and effective release of material about one's good works is vital.

Pamphlets, brochures, press releases, one's own newspaper and magazine, these and many more, must be supplied with *a comprehensible identity of self.*

Distributing or using these, one publicizes one's own good works.

And one must also *do* good works. One must, through his good works and actions at least, be visible.

So a continual, truthful and artful torrent of public relations pieces must occur.

Then one day there is no enemy.

And one's repute is high.

There may be other attacks but now one can handle them as small fires and not as a whole burning forest.

You can see that black propaganda is a covert attack on the reputation of a person, company or nation, using slander and lies in order to weaken or destroy.

Defense presupposes that the target is not that bad.

One does not have to be perfect to withstand such an attack, but it helps.

But even if one *were* perfect it would be no defense. Almost all the saints in history have been subjected to such attacks. And most of them died of it.

The answer is public relations *technology skillfully applied.*

To be skillful in anything, one has to know it and be experienced in it and *do* it.

Easing Human Relations

There is another basic element of public relations that is often overlooked and given far too little importance, but when applied correctly can give one a foundation for success in dealing with others.

The original procedure developed by man to oil the machinery of human relationships was "good manners."

Various other terms that describe this procedure are politeness, decorum, formality, etiquette, form, courtesy, refinement, polish, culture, civility, courtliness and respect.

Even the most primitive cultures had highly developed rituals of human relationship. A study of twenty-one different primitive races shows the formalities which attended their interpersonal and intertribal and interracial relationships to be quite impressive.

Throughout all races, "bad manners" are condemned.

Those with "bad manners" are *rejected.*

Thus the primary technology of public relations was "manners."

Therefore, a person or team of people applying the techniques of public relations who have not drilled and mastered the manners accepted as "good manners" by those being contacted will fail. Such a person or team may know all the senior PR technology and yet fail miserably on the sole basis of "exhibiting bad manners."

"Good manners" sum up to:

(a) granting importance to the other person and

(b) using the two-way communication cycle.

In dealing with people, it is impossible to get one's ideas across and gain any acceptance without a two-way communication cycle.

By "cycle" is meant a span of time with a beginning and an end. In a cycle of communication we have one person originating a communication to a second person who receives the communication, understands it and acknowledges it, thus ending the cycle. In a *two-way* communication cycle, the second person now originates a communication to the first person who receives it, understands it and acknowledges it. In other words, the two-way communication cycle is a normal cycle of a communication between two people. It is not a two-way communication cycle if either person fails, in his turn, to originate a communication when he should.

Whatever motions or rituals there are, these two factors—granting importance to the other person, and using the two-way communication cycle—are involved. Thus a person violating them will find himself and his program rejected.

Arrogance and force may win dominion and control but will never win acceptance and respect.

For all his "mental technology" the psychiatrist or psychologist could never win applause or general goodwill because they are personally (a) arrogant beyond belief (b) hold others in scathing contempt ("man is an animal," "people are all insane," etc.).

They just don't have "good manners"; i.e., they do not (a) consider or give others a feeling of importance and (b) they are total strangers to a communication cycle.

Successful PR

All successful public relations, then, is built upon the bedrock of good manners, as these are the first technology developed to ease human relations.

Good manners are much more widely known and respected than public relations technology. Therefore *no* public relations technology will be successful if this element is omitted.

Brushing off "mere guards" as beneath one's notice while one goes after a contact with their boss can be fatal. Who talks to their boss? These "mere guards."

Making an appointment and not keeping it, issuing an invitation too late for it to be accepted, not offering food or a drink, not standing up when a lady or important man enters, treating one's subordinates like lackeys in public, raising one's voice harshly in public, interrupting what someone else is saying to "do something important," not saying thank you or good night—these are all "bad manners." People who do these or a thousand other discourtesies are mentally rejected by those with whom they come into contact.

As public relations is basically acceptance then bad manners defeat it utterly.

To apply the techniques of PR successfully, a person has to have good manners.

This is not hard. One has to assess his attitude toward others and iron it out. Are they individually important? And then he has to have his two-way communication cycle so perfect and natural, it is never noticed.

Given those two things, a person can now learn the bits of ritual that go to make up the procedure that is considered "good manners" in the group with which he is associating.

Then given public relations technology correctly used, one has successful PR.

Importance

You have no idea how important people are. There is a reversed ratio—those at the bottom have a self-importance *far* greater than those at the top who *are* important. A charlady's (cleaning woman's) concept of her own importance is far greater than that of a successful general manager!

Ignore people at your peril.

People resent those who grant them no importance. One crucial part of "good manners" is granting importance to other people.

To see and acknowledge the existence of people is a granting of their importance.

Flattery is not very useful, is often suspect, as it does not come from a sincere belief and the falsity in it is detectable to all but a fool.

A person's importance is made evident to him by showing him respect, or just by assuring him he is visible and acceptable.

To see and acknowledge the existence of someone is a granting of their importance.

To know their name and their connections also establishes importance.

Asserting one's *own* importance is about as acceptable as a dead cat at a wedding.

People have value and are important. Big or small they are important.

If you know that, you are halfway home with good manners.

Thus public relations can occur.

Communication

The two-way communication cycle is more important than the content.

The content of the communication, the meaning to be put across to another or others, is secondary to the fact of a two-way communication cycle.

Communication exists to be replied to or used.

Communication, with the communication cycle present first, must exist before it carries any message.

Messages do not travel on no communication line. The line or route along which a communication travels from one person to another must be there.

Advertising is always violating this. "Buy Beanos!" into the empty air. Other things must establish the line. And the line must be such as to obtain an answer, either by use or purchase or reply.

A funny example was a salesman who without preamble or reason wrote to people and told them to buy a multithousand-dollar product without even an explanation of its use or value. Response zero. No communication line. He was writing to a name but not really to anyone.

In social intercourse a communication cycle must be established before any acceptance of the speaker can occur. Then one might get across a message.

A communication which travels in one direction only never establishes a two-way communication cycle. In social situations, acceptance of the person won't occur without it.

Good manners require a two-way communication cycle between oneself and the other person.

Good manners require a two-way communication cycle. This is even true of social letters and phone calls.

Out of this one gets "telling the hostess good night as one leaves."

One really has to understand the two-way communication cycle to have really good manners.

Without a two-way communication cycle, public relations is pretty poor stuff.

Rituals

If an American Indian's ritual of conference was so exact and complex, if a thousand other primitive races had precise social conduct and forms of address, then it is not too much to ask modern man to have good manners as well.

But "good manners" are less apparent in our times than they once were. This comes about because the intermingling of so many races and customs have tended to destroy the ritual patterns once well established in the smaller units.

So one appears to behold a sloppy age of manners.

This is no excuse to have bad manners.

One can have excellent manners by just observing:

a. Importance of people

b. Two-way communication cycle

c. Local rituals observed as proper conduct

These are the first musts of someone applying PR technology.

On that foundation can be built an acceptable public relations presence that makes PR succeed.

One can influence the community as a whole with public relations technology.

A survey done on sufficient numbers of the public...

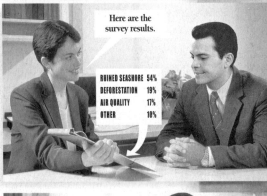

...discloses the concern that is most real to them.

A program can then be drawn up for the group that forwards their goals and which now gains community support.

The result is increased cooperation with actions that improve conditions in society and the world.

Public Relations Application

No matter how worthwhile your purpose or activity, you can't just depend on the agreement and cooperation of others. Unless your purposes are made known and real, there is little reason for others to support your efforts.

Public relations is the method one can use to get that support.

There are many PR tools available. For instance, one has surveys to discover his publics and the reality and acceptance level of each. One has the ARC triangle with the two-way cycle of communication to raise affinity and reality. There is the knowledge of manners, granting importance to others and observing their rituals, which will help one successfully interact with them.

The tools are numerous, but they must be well known and skillfully applied in order to gain the agreement of others.

There are many worthy purposes that will help this world become a better place. But no man stands alone in society, and if one wants his purposes accomplished, the cooperation of others is always necessary.

If you have a purpose to help others and improve society, you can utilize public relations to make your task easier.

Many other people have similar goals to yours, and with this technology you can reach them. Anything that is truly worthwhile is worth getting done—and you are not likely to accomplish it by yourself. PR is how you get others to work with you. ■

Practical Exercises

Here are exercises relating to public relations. Doing these will increase your understanding of the data.

1 Look around your environment and name as many different "publics" as possible. Do this until you are certain you can correctly determine various publics who would be addressed with a separate PR message.

2 Choose a specific group or public in an area or activity which you have some familiarity with. Conduct a survey on that group or public to establish their reality on some subject.

3 Tabulate the responses to the survey you did in the previous exercise, using the data in this booklet on tabulating survey responses.

4 Write down an example from your own observation or experience of the Law of the Omitted Data: "WHERE THERE IS NO DATA AVAILABLE PEOPLE WILL INVENT IT." Then give specific ways in which the person or persons involved could handle the situation using the data on PR covered in this booklet. Repeat this as many times as needed until you are certain you can correctly observe examples of the Law of the Omitted Data and know how to handle them using PR technology.

5 Find several local rituals observed as proper conduct in your area which should be observed if one is to have "good manners."

6 Go out and practice "good manners" by just observing:

        a. Importance of people

        b. Two-way communication cycle

        c. Local rituals observed as proper conduct

Do this until you can practice good manners with certainty.

RESULTS FROM APPLICATION

The technology of public relations and surveys, as developed by L. Ron Hubbard, can open any door. People who have studied this data have been amazed at its simplicity and applicability. With it, causes can be fought for and won. Ideas can be accepted where they wouldn't have been before and real production can occur unhindered. As the successes below illustrate, PR is an indispensable tool.

A woman in South America found that the female police in the city were having difficulty in getting along with the people in their district. After speaking to several of these police officers, she isolated their problem to a lack of technology on communication. She then gave a series of lectures on this subject to the female police in the city, including the basic data on "manners" and the ARC triangle. As a result she received the following acknowledgment from the Second Superintendent Commander of the Female Police who presented a plaque saying:

"In the name of the General Secretariat of Protection and Public Traffic of the Federal District Department, we acknowledge you for the valuable and altruistic promotion of the technology of L. Ron Hubbard. For giving the female police a better relationship with the citizens by the use of affinity, reality and communication, thus improving our image in the society."

A newly appointed public relations director used Scientology technology to establish goodwill for a company which had just moved to a new location. Here are his results:

"As the newly appointed public relations director for a company which had just moved to a new location, my first assignment was to establish goodwill for the company in the local community. New to the area myself, my first action was to apply L. Ron Hubbard's technology on public relations. I had surveys done in the local neighborhood to find out what the residents thought was important or needed and wanted in the area. It soon became evident that crime was of major concern and the community wanted something effective done. With this data to hand I then met with the local police. In coordination with them, I used Mr. Hubbard's data on targets and programs and worked out a neighborhood crime watch program. Volunteers from the company, who were also concerned about crime, spent a few hours each day to help implement the targets of the program by

BENEFITS OF PUBLIC RELATIONS TECHNOLOGY

The graph demonstrates what can happen when PR technology is applied. In this instance, one organization involved in training people implemented a long-range campaign to reach its public throughout a continental area, and succeeded with a substantial increase in the organization's growth.

Course Graduates

Campaign Begins

Sept. Oct. Nov. Dec. Jan. Feb. Mar. Apr. May June July

canvassing the local area getting each resident to participate in the program. Thanks to the effectiveness of this program, the crime rate in the area plummeted considerably within a matter of weeks. Not only was something actually done to handle the crime problem in that area (which was very much appreciated), but good relations with the community were established for the company as well."

Being newly employed in the complaints department of a large company became a challenge for a California woman as she found that its repair service department had broken promises to customers about the return of repaired appliances. She had studied Mr. Hubbard's technology of PR and used it to totally change the area and handle the past bad standing the company had with its customers.

"Initially I regularly got complaints. The public did not know when they would get their repairs done. That their electrical appliances were being handled in forty-eight hours was a pleasant surprise to all.

"I did have a customer on the phone at one point who had called because her appliance had been in repair for more than forty-eight hours. When I checked, I found that a special part was being gotten to improve the appearance of the appliance. I told her what was being done, where exactly the appliance was on the repair line and when she could expect it. She thanked me and was really thrilled that she was basically getting back a brand-new electrical appliance.

"I have created excellent public relations for my company—our customers now know they can trust me and my company to deliver what is promised. The managing director knows that he never has to bother about the repairs, delivery and unhandled complaints, whereas earlier these matters were always on his plate. The importance of honesty and PR is now completely real to me—this technology makes my job a pleasure."

The country of Colombia has been torn by civil violence and unrest for several years. Resolving to draw wide attention to efforts to reduce violence in their country, a group of concerned citizens utilized L. Ron Hubbard's Public Relations Technology to determine how best to make the point that violence has no part in their society. They then began a campaign to raise the level of honesty in the community, using Scientology principles of integrity and right and wrong. As a result, they got hundreds of Colombian youth gathered at an amusement park and demonstrated their desire for a country without war and violence by tossing toy guns into a fire. Their demonstration was broadcast to the entire country and had a major impact. A few weeks later, a letter was received from the president's office, endorsing the group's actions which was made known to the nation through radio and television. It said, in part:

"A few weeks later, a Colombian guerrilla group followed suit by publicly laying down their weapons (real ones),

burning them and saying no to violence, murder and destruction and saying yes to peace, happiness and survival."

A Swiss woman learned that public relations technology can be applied toward the achievement of worthwhile objectives in any aspect of life.

"When I was in college I encountered difficulty working with one of my professors. He was very difficult to talk to and seemed to be unavailable most of the time. In other circumstances I might have decided just to give up and stop taking the course. But in this case, having the information the course covered was vital to the career I had planned and I couldn't just pass it by.

"Fortunately, I was also studying Mr. Hubbard's material on public relations at the time. I realized I had before me a perfect opportunity to use the principles of PR.

"I knew that if I was to gain this man's cooperation and assistance, I would have to get into communication with him. I applied the PR principle of communicating with reality—something he could agree with, in a way that he would agree with. From observation of how he handled other students, I realized that very likely the only thing I could do to get into communication with him was to cry! So though I thought I was being a bit silly, that is exactly what I did. He immediately became concerned and interested. I had finally gotten across to him the fact that I was sincere about learning what he had to teach me, and that I truly wanted his assistance.

"With the door opened in this way, I continued to apply the principle of building reality and affinity through communication. In the end, he was strongly interested in my progress. He helped me over the difficulties I'd been having with part of the lessons, and through the rest of the course was more than willing to assist me when I had trouble grasping something.

"By the end of the course I had obtained the knowledge and ability I had come for. This would not have been possible if I had not first gained my professor's cooperation. And in fact each of us gained a friend as well."

phase of life for its author. He did, however, not cease his research, and as breakthrough after breakthrough was carefully codified through late 1951, the applied religious philosophy of Scientology was born.

Because Scientology explains the whole of life, there is no aspect of man's existence that L. Ron Hubbard's subsequent work did not address. Residing variously in the United States and England, his continued research brought forth solutions to such social ills as declining educational standards and pandemic drug abuse.

All told, L. Ron Hubbard's works on Scientology and Dianetics total forty million words of recorded lectures, books and writings. Together, these constitute the legacy of a lifetime that ended on January 24, 1986. Yet the passing of L. Ron Hubbard in no way constituted an end; for with a hundred million of his books in circulation and millions of people daily applying his technologies for betterment, it can truly be said the world still has no greater friend.■

CHURCHES OF SCIENTOLOGY

Contact Your Nearest Church or Organization or visit www.volunteerministers.org

UNITED STATES

ALBUQUERQUE
Church of Scientology
8106 Menaul Boulevard NE
Albuquerque, New Mexico
87110

ANN ARBOR
Church of Scientology
66 E. Michigan Avenue
Battle Creek, Michigan 49017

ATLANTA
Church of Scientology
1611 Mt. Vernon Road
Dunwoody, Georgia 30338

AUSTIN
Church of Scientology
2200 Guadalupe
Austin, Texas 78705

BOSTON
Church of Scientology
448 Beacon Street
Boston, Massachusetts 02115

BUFFALO
Church of Scientology
47 West Huron Street
Buffalo, New York 14202

CHICAGO
Church of Scientology
3011 North Lincoln Avenue
Chicago, Illinois 60657-4207

CINCINNATI
Church of Scientology
215 West 4th Street, 5th Floor
Cincinnati, Ohio 45202-2670

CLEARWATER
Church of Scientology
Flag Service Organization
210 South Fort Harrison Avenue
Clearwater, Florida 33756

Foundation Church of
   Scientology
Flag Ship Service Organization
c/o *Freewinds* Relay Office
118 North Fort Harrison Avenue
Clearwater, Florida 33755-4013

COLUMBUS
Church of Scientology
30 North High Street
Columbus, Ohio 43215

DALLAS
Church of Scientology
Celebrity Centre Dallas
1850 North Buckner Boulevard
Dallas, Texas 75228

DENVER
Church of Scientology
3385 South Bannock Street
Englewood, Colorado 80110

DETROIT
Church of Scientology
28000 Middlebelt Road
Farmington Hills, Michigan
48334

HONOLULU
Church of Scientology
1146 Bethel Street
Honolulu, Hawaii 96813

KANSAS CITY
Church of Scientology
3619 Broadway
Kansas City, Missouri 64111

LAS VEGAS
Church of Scientology
846 East Sahara Avenue
Las Vegas, Nevada 89104

Church of Scientology
Celebrity Centre Las Vegas
4850 W. Flamingo Road, Suite 10
Las Vegas, Nevada 89103

LONG ISLAND
Church of Scientology
99 Railroad Station Plaza
Hicksville, New York
11801-2850

LOS ANGELES AND VICINITY
Church of Scientology
   of Los Angeles
4810 Sunset Boulevard
Los Angeles, California 90027

Church of Scientology
1451 Irvine Boulevard
Tustin, California 92680

Church of Scientology
1277 East Colorado Boulevard
Pasadena, California 91106

Church of Scientology
15643 Sherman Way
Van Nuys, California 91406

Church of Scientology
American Saint Hill
   Organization
1413 L. Ron Hubbard Way
Los Angeles, California 90027

Church of Scientology
American Saint Hill Foundation
1413 L. Ron Hubbard Way
Los Angeles, California 90027

Church of Scientology
Advanced Organization
   of Los Angeles
1306 L. Ron Hubbard Way
Los Angeles, California 90027

Church of Scientology
Celebrity Centre International
5930 Franklin Avenue
Hollywood, California 90028

LOS GATOS
Church of Scientology
2155 South Bascom Avenue,
   Suite 120
Campbell, California 95008

MIAMI
Church of Scientology
120 Giralda Avenue
Coral Gables, Florida 33134

MINNEAPOLIS
Church of Scientology
Twin Cities
1011 Nicollet Mall
Minneapolis, Minnesota 55403

MOUNTAIN VIEW
Church of Scientology
2483 Old Middlefield Way
Mountain View, California
94043

NASHVILLE
Church of Scientology
Celebrity Centre Nashville
1204 16th Avenue South
Nashville, Tennessee 37212

NEW HAVEN
Church of Scientology
909 Whalley Avenue
New Haven, Connecticut
06515-1728

NEW YORK CITY
Church of Scientology
227 West 46th Street
New York, New York
10036-1409

Church of Scientology
Celebrity Centre New York
65 East 82nd Street
New York, New York 10028

ORLANDO
Church of Scientology
1830 East Colonial Drive
Orlando, Florida 32803-4729

PHILADELPHIA
Church of Scientology
1315 Race Street
Philadelphia, Pennsylvania
19107

PHOENIX
Church of Scientology
2111 West University Drive
Mesa, Arizona 85201

PORTLAND
Church of Scientology
2636 NE Sandy Boulevard
Portland, Oregon 97232-2342

Church of Scientology
Celebrity Centre Portland
708 SW Salmon Street
Portland, Oregon 97205

SACRAMENTO
Church of Scientology
825 15th Street
Sacramento, California
95814-2096

SALT LAKE CITY
Church of Scientology
1931 South 1100 East
Salt Lake City, Utah 84106

SAN DIEGO
Church of Scientology
1330 4th Avenue
San Diego, California 92101

SAN FRANCISCO
Church of Scientology
83 McAllister Street
San Francisco, California 94

SAN JOSE
Church of Scientology
80 East Rosemary Street
San Jose, California 95112

SANTA BARBARA
Church of Scientology
524 State Street
Santa Barbara, California 93

SEATTLE
Church of Scientology
2226 3rd Avenue
Seattle, Washington 98121

ST. LOUIS
Church of Scientology
6901 Delmar Boulevard
University City, Missouri 63

TAMPA
Church of Scientology
3617 Henderson Boulevard
Tampa, Florida 33609-4501

WASHINGTON, DC
Founding Church of Scient
   of Washington, DC
1701 20th Street NW
Washington, DC 20009

PUERTO RICO

HATO REY
Dianetics Center of Puerto
272 JT Piñero Avenue
Hyde Park
San Juan, Puerto Rico 0091

CANADA

EDMONTON
Church of Scientology
10206 106th Street NW
Edmonton, Alberta
Canada T5J 1H7